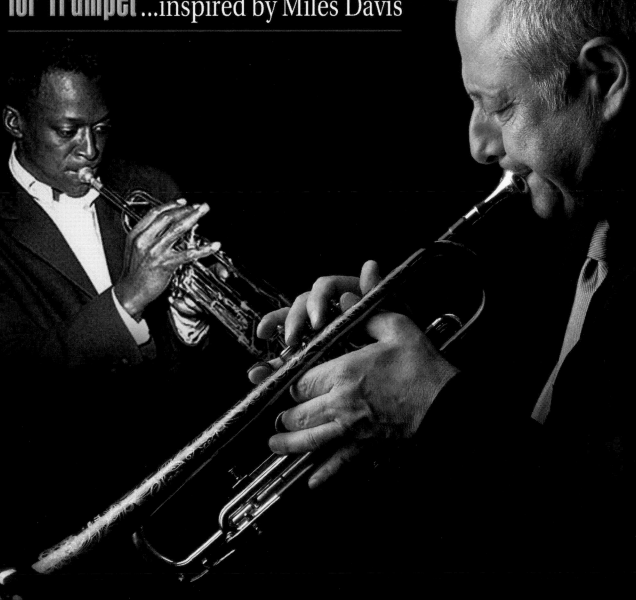

12230

Glenn Zottola

All-Star Band plus
Orchestral Backgrounds
for Trumpet ...inspired by Miles Davis

- notes continued from back cover

Two of the first three tracks captures Zottola on the muted horn starting out with a dynamic rendition of the Harry Warren composition **"This Heart of Mine"** while the Jimmy Raney piece *"Jupiter,"* features the trumpeter on a Davis-styled fast-paced romp attesting to this trumpeter's more than appreciable chops on the instrument. The Sammy Fain jazz standard **"I'll Be Seeing You,"** is the first of the large orchestrations capturing the emotional power of a song that became an anthem for soldiers serving during the Second World War, here Zottola's warmed-toned trumpet provides a solemn sound on a beautiful ballad of some historical significance.

Included here is the 1933 Johnny Green chart **"I Cover the Waterfront,"** played straight by Zottola, it's a melancholy almost somber piece of music where Zottola's trumpet voice takes center stage on the album's most down tempo track. On this piece, the trumpeter infuses a quote at the end of the tune from French Composer Leo Delibes' **"The Maids of Cadiz,"** taken from the 1957 album *Miles Ahead,* an album which left an impression on the young Zottola and marked the very first collaboration between Davis and arranger Gil Evans. By contrast, the Rodgers and Hart standard **"Spring Is Here,"** enjoys a bouncy mid-tempo burn where Zottola's muted horn is accompanied well by the sounds of the guitar and the splashing brushes in another small ensemble format.

Though not a Davis composition, the Raney tune **"Beta Minus,"** sure sounds like it may have emanated from the legend's songbook and while brief, the leader does an excellent job of projecting the Davis style with his playful horn-play. Recorded countless times by many artists, the familiar jazz standard **"Autumn in New York"** makes another appearance here, this time presented with a spacious string arrangement pronouncing the trumpet in a gorgeous treatment of the classic where once again, he employs another trumpet quote from **"The Maids of Cadiz"** affirming the influence the Davis/Evans album continues to have on this artist. Theloneous Monk's famous 1948 **"Evidence,"** is actually a contra fact of Jesse Greer's 1929 **"Just You Just Me"** which is just the type of perky tune someone like Davis would be drawn to. Zottola performs the piece in a small group setting sounding off with a bit more power play than on the other songs.

Sounding very much like the legend himself, Zottola provides his last take on the muted horn blowing a mesmerizing rendition of the show piece song from the 1937 musical "Babes in Arms," known to everyone as the Rodgers and Hart popular standard **"My Funny Valentine,"** on this track, when you listen closely to the voice of this trumpet, it's like hearing Davis himself. The tribute closes out with a rousing read of the 1926 Jule Styne/Ned Miller composition **"Sunday,"** where the trumpeter finalizes his tribute playing with a quartet alongside the voice of the saxophone, guitarist and crashing cymbal accents from the drummer—just like how Davis would plan to go out.

Miles Davis was a lyrical trumpeter who popularized a multi-styled approach to the trumpet revolutionizing the jazz world. This album is much more than a musical homage to a master of the instrument and a pioneer of the genre, it is a personal remembrance of a musician who had more influence on Glenn Zottola than he had previously thought. As Glenn states, this offering is not an attempt to sound just like Davis, only to reimagine the style that has influenced his view of the music and the way he plays the trumpet today. On this album, Zottola succeeds quite well in recreating the spirit and flavor of Davis style and does so in his own unique way. Miles Davis is well remembered on this fitting tribute, but what may be surprising to listeners of this album, is just how well one may remember Zottola!

Edward Blanco
Producer and host at WDNA, 88.9FM jazz
radio in Miami and writer with All About Jazz.

All-Star Band plus Orchestral Backgrounds

CONTENTS

All songs transcribed and engraved by Mark Lopeman

ISBN 978-1-941566-93-0

SOLO Bb TRUMPET

This Heart of Mine

music by
Harry Warren
lyrics by
Arthur Freed

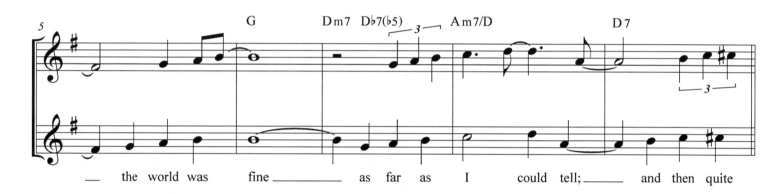

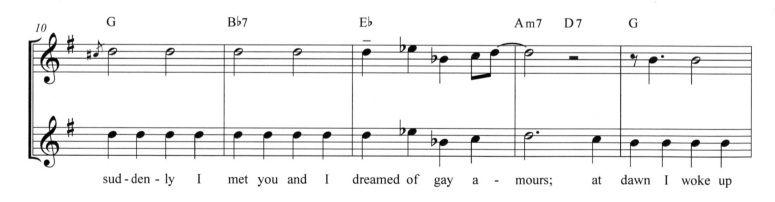

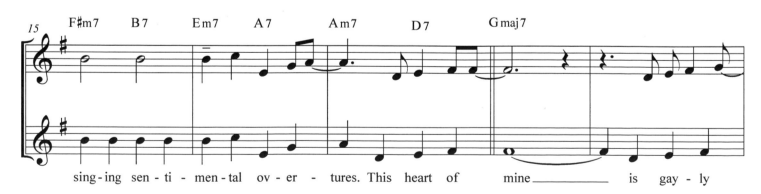

SOLO Bb TRUMPET

I'll Be Seeing You

music by
Sammy Fain
lyrics by
Irving Kahal

GLENN'S SOLO

SOLO Bb TRUMPET

Jupiter

composed by
Jimmy Raney

MELODY ("HEAD")

MMO 12230

SOLO Bb TRUMPET

I Cover the Waterfront

music by
Johnny Green
lyrics by
Edward Heyman

GLENN'S SOLO

A

ORIG. MELODY

0:17

I cov-er the wat - er - front,   I'm watch-ing the

sea,   will the one I love⸺ be com - ing back to

B

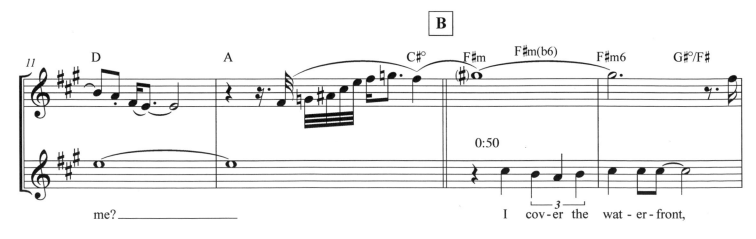

0:50

me?⸺   I cov - er the wat - er - front,

SOLO Bb TRUMPET

Spring Is Here

music by
Richard Rodgers
lyrics by
Lorenz Hart

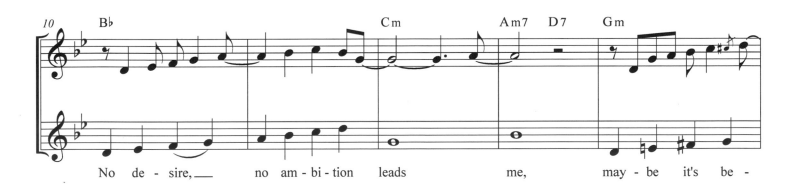

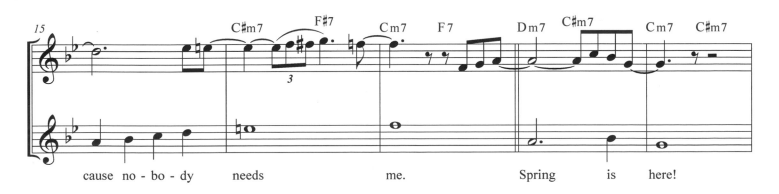

MMO 12230

19

MMO 12230

SOLO Bb TRUMPET

Beta Minus

composed by
Jimmy Raney

MMO 12230

SOLO Bb TRUMPET

Autumn in New York

music and lyrics by
Vernon Duke

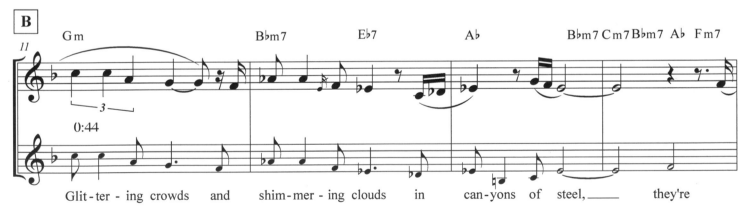

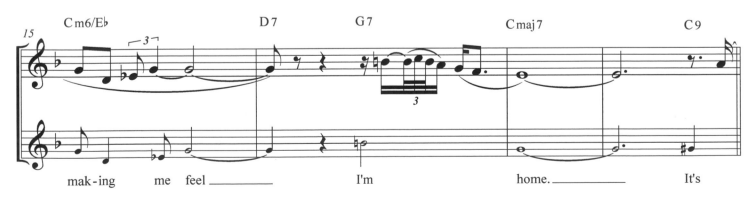

MMO 12230

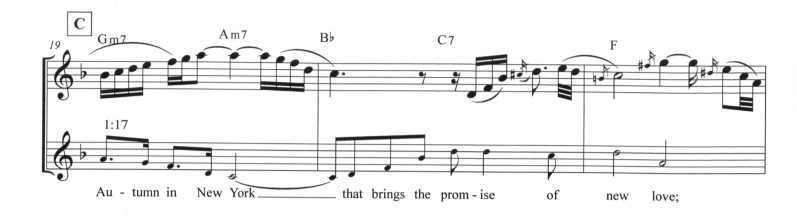

SOLO Bb TRUMPET

Just You, Just Me

music by
Jesse Greer
lyrics by
Raymond Klages

(Sax)

A MELODY ("HEAD")

FM7　F7　Bb　Bbm6

0:10 ORIG. MELODY

Just you, just me, Let's find a co-zy spot,

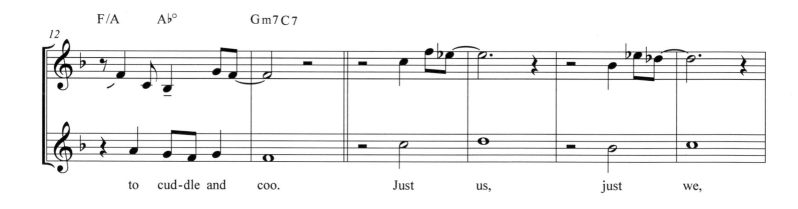

F/A　Ab°　Gm7 C7

to cud-dle and coo. Just us, just we,

FM7　F7　Bb　Bbm6　F　Cm7　F7

I've missed an aw-ful lot, my trou-ble is you. Oh, gee!

What are your charms ___ for? What are my arms for? Use your im -

ag - i - na - tion! Just you, just me,

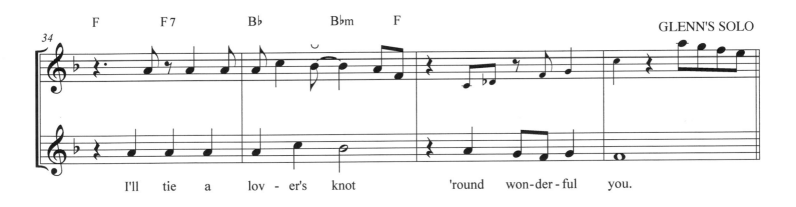

GLENN'S SOLO

I'll tie a lov - er's knot 'round won-der-ful you.

B

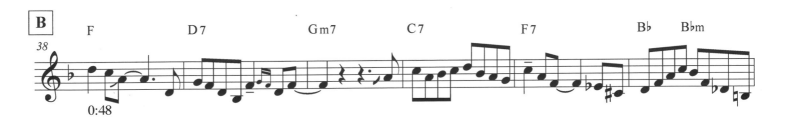

0:48

SOLO Bb TRUMPET

My Funny Valentine

music by
Richard Rodgers
lyrics by
Lorenz Hart

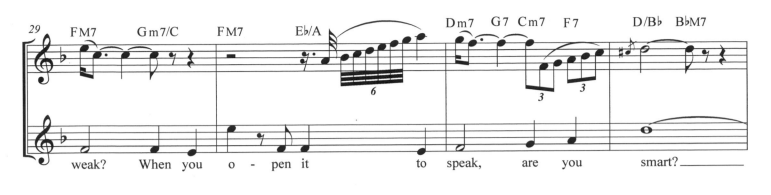

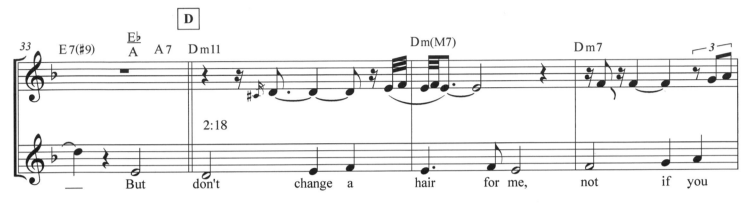

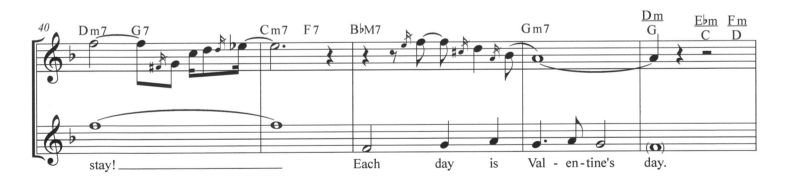

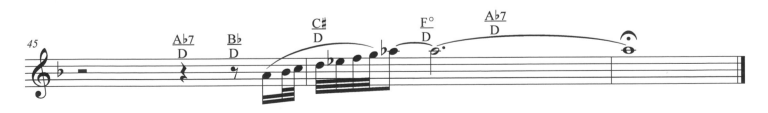

SOLO Bb TRUMPET

Sunday

words and music by
Ned Miller
Chester Cohn
Jule Styne
Bennie Kreuger

Music Minus One
50 Executive Boulevard • Elmsford, New York 10523-1325
914-592-1188 • e-mail: info@musicminusone.com
www.musicminusone.com

MMO 12230

ISBN 978-1-941566-93-0